SONS OF GOD

LONNA HARDIN

SONGBIRD PUBLISHING

FEEL THE TREMORS

A 7.7 magnitude earthquake struck two days ago between Cuba and Jamaica. In January 2020, 9,888 total earthquakes were recorded around the world (2020, volcanodiscovery.com). Earthquakes have been around since the beginning of time.

To the average eye, it appears as though all is business as usual. It may seem as if nothing is happening out of the norm, but I beg to differ. Why are earthquakes occurring more frequently? Show more statistics to prove this statement. Why is the time between quakes getting shorter and shorter? Why now? I'll tell you why, the earth is groaning and moaning waiting for the manifestation of the sons of God.

It was 2003, and my Mother had just suffered a brain aneurysm that ruptured the year before. All hell had seemingly broken out in my life and family. Nothing was working out as planned. A year earlier, all seemed to be heading in the right direction in my life.

I was young, beautiful, and single. I worked for my church. I was the youth administrator helping coordinate youth conferences, services, and events. I lived in a small town named Battle Creek, but traveled throughout the U.S. going to conventions, concerts, and more.

I had the favor of my Pastor. I had the love and comfort of a church congregation. I had a dream to sing around the world and a passion for the Lord. What I did not have is any idea how my life was about to change.

It was October 2, 2002 when I received the call. My Mother had been rushed to Bronson Hospital for emergency surgery. While teaching a cell group bible study, her blood pressure had risen to dangerous levels. As a result, her brain aneurysm ruptured and she suffered a stroke on each side of her brain. It was a devastating call that no 27-year-old should have to receive.

I rushed home to Kalamazoo to meet my sisters at the hospital. It was the last time I heard my Mother speak in a voice that was familiar. She was calling on the name of Jesus and told us to go and get her financial papers. She wanted to make sure that what she had built was protected and secure.

Scared and not knowing what to do, my sisters and I felt helpless as to what was about to happen. For the next three weeks we would wait in prayer and expectation as my Mother's life hung in the balance. We watched her being intubated on a life support machine while we fought through diagnosis after diagnosis, pain after pain.

When the danger period was over and she needed rehabilitation, we would travel to and from the hospital for five months, thanking God for every additional day. We would praise Him for another chance to get it right and for sparing our mother's life.

In my own personal life, I spent time reflecting every day. No one knew, but I went without gas and heat for one year. I gave back the car I had. I lived on rice because nothing mattered to me at that point but my family.

I spent the summer of 2003 interceding for my family. I cried out every day alone in an empty apartment, begging God to turn the tides. I repented for our transgressions and wept before the Lord.

At that time, I didn't care about anything else. Nothing seemed to matter. In the process, I lost my job, but I didn't care. During this season, I also lost a long-time mentor who I had known since the age of 18, and an Uncle who had been our rock during this tragic time.

It was a season of loss. It was a season of mourning. It was a season of grieving what used to be and rejecting what was. It was a season of devastation. It was a time of losing friends who walked away because they couldn't see what was going on behind the scenes.

When I started to become more introverted and withdrawn, there was no one there but God. During this time there were some things that happened in our family, and we couldn't tell a soul. They were too embarrassing. They seemed humiliating and against everything we knew our Mother stood for.

Looking back, I can see God's hand in it all. I must admit, at the time I didn't see it and couldn't understand what was going on. I felt ashamed. I felt demeaned. I felt forsaken by God and persecuted. It was a Garden of Gethsemane experience that felt like it lasted a lifetime.

There was a time when I couldn't talk or write about these things without tears streaming down my face. This was such a tender time. It was a time of brokenness and rejection. It was a time of isolation and crushing. God had me right where he needed me to be.

In 2003, I auditioned for the theatre program at Western Michigan University. I passed the audition and was accepted into the school. I majored in theatre and minored in musical theatre. I was in action, pursuing my lifelong dreams. Still, because my Mother was married at the time, chaos was happening all around.

I remember one day walking around campus. I had just come from my Mother's house and had been praying and warring all night about some things that were going on. As I walked, I started to hear a melody. Then, I started to sing. God was giving me a battle song. It went like this:

Far Above, Principalities,
Far Above, The Rulers of the darkness of this world,
Far Above, Spiritual Wickedness so high,
That's where I'm seated, that's where I'm seated,
I'm seated in You.

More words to the song came and I continued to sing. Every note I sang enforced my new declaration. "That's where I'm seated, that's where I'm seated, I'm seated in you."

More and more songs kept coming. These songs were being birthed out of my pain. They were birthed out of a life changing experience that revealed new dimensions of God to me. The revelations exposed through these songs have long been ignored by the Body of Christ.

Now, the earth is ready and waiting. The earth travails for the manifestation of the Sons of God (Romans 8:19). The problem is many believers can't access this promise or walk in this revelation because many still struggle with their identity.

I have friends throughout the world. If you count the connections on my social channels, you would think my life was an open book. The truth is, most of my life I have struggled with my identity. I was gifted, kind, and what some would call charismatic. However, the truth is I grew up without truly knowing my Father.

My Father was a preacher. I would see him from time to time, but not very often. My earliest memory of him was when I was about five years old. If he was around before that, I don't remember. When he would come around, he would give us money or take us out to eat. Then, before you could take it all in, he would be gone.

When my Father passed in March 2017, I heard story after story of what a great man he was. We became very close during the last 20 years of his life, but the truth is, I spent most of my childhood years feeling out of place and that a huge void was missing from my life.

I share this because many have a similar experience. Many are like I was, lost without direction and lacking identity. It wasn't until I matured in Christ that I began to find myself. These illuminations in him allowed me to see who I was in him and who he was calling me to be.

Tragically, I made devastating mistakes on the road to discovery. Some of these errors could have deterred my vision. Others could have sabotaged my destiny, but God in his goodness and loving kindness said, "No." He intercepted and defeated the plans of the enemy.

He spoke the following passage over my life and today, He is speaking it over you:

JEREMIAH 29:11-14 KJV

11 For I know the thoughts that I think toward you, saith the Lord, thoughts of peace, and not of evil, to give you an expected end.

12 Then shall ye call upon me, and ye shall go and pray unto me, and I will hearken unto you.

13 And ye shall seek me, and find me, when ye shall search for me with all your heart.

14 And I will be found of you, saith the Lord: and I will turn away your captivity, and I will gather you from all the nations, and from all the places whither I have driven you, saith the Lord; and I will bring you again into the place whence I caused you to be carried away captive.

As I look back, I often wonder, What if I had found my calling much sooner? What if all the mistakes and missteps could have been avoided? Would my life look differently if I had someone to validate what I felt inside all along? My answer is a resounding, Yes!

Although I can never go back and change my life, I can surely help someone else along the way. I can share the lessons and concepts revealed to me along the way. I can empower someone else to take a step closer to their divine destiny. The truth is, although it is great to be loved and accepted, we are the ones obligated to deliver the goods.

God leaves the responsibility of utilizing our full potential solely on our shoulders. We have to take up our own cross and carry this burden. Sometimes it means walking alone. Sometimes it means coming to the harsh reality that if anything is going to happen in our lives, it is because we find faith, take action, and move ahead.

My prayer is that as you read the following pages, you are divinely positioned to answer earth's groan. Someone somewhere is waiting for you to show up. You have been uniquely and exquisitely created for such a time as this. Will you answer the call?

LUKE 12:48 KJV

48 But he that knew not, and did commit things worthy of stripes, shall be beaten with few stripes. For unto whomsoever much is given, of him shall be much required: and to whom men have committed much, of him they will ask the more.

TWENTY YEARS ago when I heard that scripture I cringed. I felt like it was a death sentence, a painful agony that only a few had to go through. No one explained that this journey to and on the cross was one every believer had to make. I thought I was special and unique.

MATTHEW 7:13-14 KJV

13 Enter ye in at the strait gate: for wide is the gate, and broad is the way, that leadeth to destruction, and many there be which go in thereat:

14 Because strait is the gate, and narrow is the way, which leadeth unto life, and few there be that find it.

LOOKING BACK, I now see there was nothing really special about me. What was special is the less traveled road I found myself on. I was looking for life. I was looking for a "straight" and "narrow" way. What I discovered is that no matter what path brought you to this place, it all led to one thing: Making a decision to carry your cross.

MATTHEW 16:24-35 KJV

24 Then said Jesus unto his disciples, If any man will come after me, let him deny himself, and take up his cross, and follow me.

25 For whosoever will save his life shall lose it: and whosoever will lose his life for my sake shall find it.

SONSHIP

The cross of Christ gets heavy sometimes. Your cross is normally equal to the glory that will be revealed in you. Christ was rejected. Fellow Jews spit in his face. He often had to steal away to spare his life.

Who told us the road would be easy? Who said salvation was for the faint of heart? Who said wearing the title, "Christian" and going to church was all you needed to make it in? Whoever it was surely lied!

We live in a society that has painted being a Christian as a social club for an elite, select few. Worse, because of this false image, there are many who have gone through hard suffering and persecutions sitting on the side feeling alone, abandoned, and as if they don't count.

These are the ones believing God's word, but rarely seeing it demonstrated when interacting with someone who claims to be His. You know what I mean don't you? Those that say, "Honor the Pastor and pray for your leaders," but ignore the part about what happens if and when you offend one of His sheep?

LUKE 17:1-2 KJV

17 Then said he unto the disciples, It is impossible but that offences will come: but woe unto him, through whom they come!

2 It were better for him that a millstone were hanged about his neck, and he cast into the sea, than that he should offend one of these little ones.

OR WHAT ABOUT those who preach, "Do not forsake the assembly of yourselves?" Or, when they talk about how important it is to tithe and give, while never preaching against the oppression of the poor.

This imbalance in the Body of Christ has caused many to leave the church, turn their back on God, give up hope, and God is not pleased. I have always lived by this scripture:

JAMES 1:27 KJV

27 Pure religion and undefiled before God and the Father is this, To visit the fatherless and widows in their affliction, and to keep himself unspotted from the world.

WHEN I WAS YOUNGER, I didn't ask questions. I took this scripture to mean exactly what it said. As I became older, I really wanted to understand God's mind. Last year I was seated in a business conference, and the Spirit of God spoke to me so clearly:

"You're interceding for the fatherless and the widow"

SPECIAL PLACE IN GOD'S HEART

I was so totally taken off guard, that I looked around startled. I pulled out my iPhone to take notes. He (God) shared more. The fatherless and widow are those who are uncovered, unprovided for, and uncared for. They lack a name or identity.

He went on to reveal they had a "Special place in His heart." So much opened up and unintentionally, I built my business on this principle. A love for this select group has been ingrained in me for a very long time.

A few years earlier, I had specifically asked God about the above-mentioned scripture in James 1:27. He shared how much He hates fatherlessness. Seeking to understand more about why, He divulged:

"Fatherlessness perverts the image of God."

When Jesus taught the Lord's prayer, He started with, "Our Father, which art in Heaven." This revealed relationship—which was God's original intent. He wanted Adam to see Him as provider, protector, and Father in the garden. When Adam and Eve ruled the earth, they were literally covered with the glory of God.

God's promises are tied to sonship. All authority in Heaven and earth has been given to sons.

MATTHEW 28:18-20 KJV

18 And Jesus came and spake unto them, saying, All power is given unto me in heaven and in earth.

19 Go ye therefore, and teach all nations, baptizing them in the name of the Father, and of the Son, and of the Holy Ghost:

20 Teaching them to observe all things whatsoever I have commanded you: and, lo, I am with you always, even unto the end of the world. Amen.

I'VE ALWAYS HAD a relationship with God and He has revealed so much to me. In the past, I haven't shared much unless it was with my closest circle. I've never been one to say, "God said," or proclaim to be a "Prophet." The bible says:

DEUTERONOMY 18:22 KJV

22 When a prophet speaketh in the name of the Lord, if the thing follow not, nor come to pass, that is the thing which the Lord hath not spoken, but the prophet hath spoken it presumptuously: thou shalt not be afraid of him.

I'VE BEEN reluctant to step out and discuss revelations or things shared from time spent in my quiet place. I only share now for purpose. It is for a time such as this. Let's look at the importance of sonship further.

When I first gave my life back to the Lord, I would talk to Him about the simplest things. One day after reading God's word, this scripture kept coming back to me:

MATTHEW 5:17-18 KJV

17 Think not that I am come to destroy the law, or the prophets: I am not come to destroy, but to fulfil.

18 For verily I say unto you, Till heaven and earth pass, one jot or one tittle shall in no wise pass from the law, till all be fulfilled.

I KEPT HEARING this in my head, but I didn't quite understand it. I know Jesus said he came to fulfill the law, but what did that mean? God spoke clearly. "Before Jesus all man saw was the law. He didn't understand the purpose of the law. Jesus was the why. He was the love behind the law."

In other words, all man saw was the law. All man saw was the "Thou shalt not." Man did not see that the reason God said, "Thou shalt not," was because if you did, you would surely die."

We should serve God out of love and passion to draw closer to Him, not out of obligation or being forced. We are His. It is because

"His love is shed abroad in our hearts." What does this have to do with sonship you ask?

SONSHIP IS ABOUT POSITIONING

Sonship is about positioning. It's about relationship. It's about knowing the Father's voice. It's about following His lead. It's about reigning on God's throne.

Sons obey God's commands because they know the rules of the house. So many miss Sonship. They're birthed into the Kingdom, but are blinded by where they find themselves. They live a false image based on where they've been, not upon whose they are.

When you're truly a believer, you're born into a family—a body of believers. You become a citizen of Heaven. You no longer are someone running "to and fro" lacking purpose or identity. This is critical.

COLOSSIANS 3:17 KJV

17 And whatsoever ye do in word or deed, do all in the name of the Lord Jesus, giving thanks to God and the Father by him.

FOLLOWING THE FOOTSTEPS OF JESUS

Why? In the 90s, there was a popular saying, "What would Jesus do?" It was a phenomenon that made millions. You'll find scripture after scripture of Jesus teaching on doing things in "His name." Whether casting out devils, salvation, receiving a child, baptizing, miracles or more. Jesus says, "Do it in my name."

Name denotes character. Names have meaning. In some cultures, they are given to reflect what you will become or what you represent. Jesus is saying, "Whatever you do, do it in my character". What is Jesus' character?

ST. JOHN 5:19-20 KJV

19 Then answered Jesus and said unto them, Verily, verily, I say unto you, The Son can do nothing of himself, but what he seeth the Father do: for what things soever he doeth, these also doeth the Son likewise.

20 For the Father loveth the Son, and sheweth him all things that himself doeth: and he will shew him greater works than these, that ye may marvel.

JESUS DID the will of the Father. He had a humble heart. His life was solely built on hearing God's voice and following His command. This is the lifestyle of the believer. It is the lifestyle of every son.

JAMES 1:22 KJV

22 BUT BE ye doers of the word, and not hearers only, deceiving your own selves.

SONSHIP ISN'T CLAIMED, IT IS AFFIRMED

MATTHEW 3:17 KJV

17 And lo a voice from heaven, saying, This is my beloved Son, in whom I am well pleased.

SONSHIP ISN'T something that can be claimed by any and everyone. It must be affirmed. I remember experiencing years of rebellion and church hurt. As a young woman, I grew up without my Father. I never really knew or understood the pure love of a man. Ever since I was a little girl, I dreamed of being married. What I was really looking for was someone to fill an empty void. I wanted to hear a man's voice affirming me.

I developed a prayer life as a child. After dedicating my life to God in my early 20's, regular church attendance became my lifestyle. I remember seeking God. I carried the heart of my Pastor and church. I would pray about it because I really saw My former Pastor as my Father.

One day, my pastor stopped me after church to tell me that God told him in prayer that "I was a real daughter" to him. Joy filled my soul. I was so grateful for God's confirmation. I had given my young adult days to serving, and knowing God was hearing my prayers was everything.

I wish I could say the story ended there, but it didn't. As the years went on, things changed. My Pastor and I grew more and more apart. He was going through transition. I was going through spiritual warfare. Our conversations were no longer the same. Things he would say to me, crushed my spirit. Looking back, I realize it wasn't intentional. However, I often wondered if he even remembered what God said.

God began taking me on a personal journey of sonship (even though I'm his daughter). Although God used a man to confirm some things, He knew that putting your confidence in man and trusting in flesh will leave you vulnerable to the enemy. So over a period of time, God began to affirm me because He knew I needed it.

God had to confirm my identity. He had to affirm who I was. He needed me so completely confident of who I was in Him, that no one could shake my faith or trust in Him.

ST. JOHN 10:27-30 KJV

27 My sheep hear my voice, and I know them, and they follow me:

28 And I give unto them eternal life; and they shall never perish, neither shall any man pluck them out of my hand.

29 My Father, which gave them me, is greater than all; and no man is able to pluck them out of my Father's hand.

30 I and my Father are one.

GOD IS RAISING SONS; though some have been rejected, some abused, and others abandoned. Regardless, they're still His sons. The earth waits for them to show up in the fullness of God's power and glory.

Many are like me. I was in church, going Sunday after Sunday. God was speaking to me and revealing things. He was showing me things to come. My faith was increasing. I was taking steps going from glory to glory and faith to faith.

All was well. I was on track for one of the greatest breakthroughs and blessings of walking in my calling. Then, I took my eyes off God and started putting my confidence in man.

GET YOUR EYES AND HEART SET BACK ON GOD!

PSALMS 118:8-9 KJV

8 It is better to trust in the Lord than to put confidence in man.
   9 It is better to trust in the Lord than to put confidence in princes.

YOU ARE AFFIRMED

$\mathcal{L}$ ooking back, I see that I was looking for affirmation. I was looking for a man or woman to confirm what God put in my heart. That search cost me 20 years of my life. Instead of stepping out to do God's will, I was caught up in pleasing man looking for a stamp of approval.

Many in the Body of Christ are in this exact state. They are looking for the voice of affirmation. Like me, they didn't have it as a child. They were without a father figure to show them who they are, or teach them who they were called to be.

THIS INTERNAL EMPTINESS **or void has them looking for validation in:**

1. Sex & Pornography
2. Drugs & Alcohol
3. Violence & Abuse
4. Money, Status, & Fame
5. Food & Overeating
6. Religion & Spirituality

7. Material Things

I know I searched for God in some of those things. I had a deep craving and longing for God in my soul. I looked for it in the church instead of God. When the church didn't satisfy my appetite, I began searching in other things. Attempting to fill empty voids with earthly, sensual vices cripples sonship.

2 CORINTHIANS 2:11 KJV

11 Lest Satan should get an advantage of us: for we are not ignorant of his devices.

LIKE THE PRODIGAL SON, many have "wasted their substance on riotous living" (Luke 15:13). Are you caught in a pigpen? Do you wonder, "How in the world you got there?" Then it's time to locate yourself. It's time to come home and get back to who you truly are, or find out who God has called you to be!

LUKE 15:17-22 KJV

17 And when he came to himself, he said, How many hired servants of my father's have bread enough and to spare, and I perish with hunger!

18 I will arise and go to my father, and will say unto him, Father, I have sinned against heaven, and before thee,

19 And am no more worthy to be called thy son: make me as one of thy hired servants.

20 And he arose, and came to his father. But when he was yet a great way off, his father saw him, and had compassion, and ran, and fell on his neck, and kissed him.

21 And the son said unto him, Father, I have sinned against heaven, and in thy sight, and am no more worthy to be called thy son.

22 But the father said to his servants, Bring forth the best robe, and put it on him; and put a ring on his hand, and shoes on his feet:

. . .

IN THIS SEASON, God is affirming you. He is saying:

"DO NOT LOOK TO MAN. **Find what you need in me. I called you. I chose you before the foundation of the world for my purposes and to reveal my glory."**

To affirm means: State as fact; assert strongly and publicly (dictionary.com/affirm).

God wants to affirm you so you will know who you are, so the world will know you are His. He wants to affirm you so they can see a reflection of God in the earth. He wants the world to see a creation that walks and talks like God.

I JOHN 3:2 KJV

2 Beloved, now are we the sons of God, and it doth not yet appear what we shall be: but we know that, when he shall appear, we shall be like him; for we shall see him as he is.

WHEN THE WORLD SEES US, they are supposed to see the Sons of God walking in the fullness of Sonship. In my book titled, "Lord of Economic Kingdoms," I discuss the many dimensions of God. Sons see those dimensions. They have up and close personal encounters with the Father.

Sons see God's authority, dominion, and commandments. They see the Father's creativity. They see their Daddy's correction. They see His compassion. More than anything, they see Him in themselves living on the inside. They hear His voice leading them. Everything sons do points back to the Father.

ROMANS 8:14 KJV

8 So then they that are in the flesh cannot please God.

9 But ye are not in the flesh, but in the Spirit, if so be that the Spirit of God dwell in you. Now if any man have not the Spirit of Christ, he is none of his.

10 And if Christ be in you, the body is dead because of sin; but the Spirit is life because of righteousness.

11 But if the Spirit of him that raised up Jesus from the dead dwell in you, he that raised up Christ from the dead shall also quicken your mortal bodies by his Spirit that dwelleth in you.

12 Therefore, brethren, we are debtors, not to the flesh, to live after the flesh.

13 For if ye live after the flesh, ye shall die: but if ye through the Spirit do mortify the deeds of the body, ye shall live.

14 For as many as are led by the Spirit of God, they are the sons of God.

1 JOHN 3:2 tells us, "Now are we the sons of God," so what are we waiting for? God says, "The time is now for sons to arise!" Arise to righteousness. Arise to holiness. Arise to dominion. Arise to authority. Arise, arise, arise!

So many are looking for the return of Jesus Christ. He isn't coming back until His sons arise and conquer the earth. The Father seeks a full harvest resulting from our labor, and His children bearing fruit!

MARK 12:2-9 KJV

2 And at the season he sent to the husbandmen a servant, that he might receive from the husbandmen of the fruit of the vineyard.

3 And they caught him, and beat him, and sent him away empty.

4 And again he sent unto them another servant; and at him they cast stones, and wounded him in the head, and sent him away shamefully handled.

5 And again he sent another; and him they killed, and many others; beating some, and killing some.

6 Having yet therefore one son, his well beloved, he sent him also last unto them, saying, They will reverence my son.

7 But those husbandmen said among themselves, This is the heir; come, let us kill him, and the inheritance shall be ours.'

8 And they took him, and killed him, and cast him out of the vineyard.

9 What shall therefore the lord of the vineyard do? he will come and destroy the husbandmen, and will give the vineyard unto others.

BELOVED, now is the time. Wickedness and unrighteousness is at an all-time high. Suicide is on the rise. Darkness is attempting to linger on the face of the earth. The Spirit of the Lord is saying in this hour, "Let there be light!" It is time for the church to arise and our light to shine!

In a lost "selfies world" of iPads, iPhones, and iPods, it is important to remember that in Christ, it is not about "I" at all. We should not allow ourselves to get caught up in the sea of social media likes. It's time to do a quick sonship "I" check.

REPEAT AFTER ME:

- *I put on Christ*
- *I am hidden in Christ*
- *In Him I live, I move, and I have my being*
- *I am crucified with Christ*
- *I allow Christ to live in me.*
- *I decrease so God can increase.*
- *I put on the whole armor of God*
- *I am a Son of the Most High God!*
- *I manifest sonship now!*

Sonship always points back to the Father.

IT REFLECTS HIS GLORY, authority, love, and forgiveness. Many are lost in sin as a result of the absence of sonship.

SONSHIP RELEASES **the three I's:**

1. **Identity** - Who You Are
2. **Image** - What You See
3. **Inheritance** - What You Will Get

Say this with me, *"I am a son of the Most High God!"*

We were born into the world to be sons (and daughters) of God. If you choose to settle for anything less, you are living beneath your privilege. The world system loves for you to settle for crumbs, forget who you are leaving your inheritance on the table.

As long as you don't know who and whose you are, your world will continue in chaos. Additionally, oppression will continue to rule the day. Many who need hope will be lost looking for love in all the wrong places. It is time to rise up, proclaim your identity, claim your inheritance, and take back what was stolen from you!

IDENTITY CRISIS

In 2002, I helped coordinate our church youth conference. Our theme was, "Mirror, Mirror." Youth could relate to a discussion about their own reflection in the mirror, versus how others saw them. I'll never forget how powerful and life changing this event was. We had young people attend from all over the U.S.

What stood out is that most young people looked to something outside to define who they were. They found their identity in their family, local church, the media, or friends. Because of this, many couldn't effectively articulate the pressures they were facing or things they were going through. They were relating to others with no expectation of being related to.

After the conference, many began to see themselves through a different set of eyes. They also became empowered with the knowledge that no one else gets to translate who or what they see in the mirror. The power to take a hard look at what and who they were was completely in their hands.

This discovery process helped each to begin a journey on truly recognizing, embracing, and celebrating their identity. Taking ownership liberated, freed, and helped them show up much more intentionally and powerfully.

When you don't recognize who you are, no one else can either. When you don't show up and identify what you stand for and what you're about, you are left clinging to a false identity. I call this having a spiritual identity crisis.

It is evident this crisis is happening in our world today. People are confused about their gender, many churches lack power, husbands and wives are running from responsibility, and many men and women don't understand their worth.

I remember when I went through my own identity crisis. It lasted approximately 15 years after I experienced church hurt and my mother had the brain aneurysm. I felt misunderstood and alone. I wanted to walk away from everything I knew and believed. I was very angry.

I didn't understand why so many negative things were happening in succession. Everyone knew me as the strong, vibrant, happy person. All of that was gone—I was depleted and sad. I felt like giving up, but couldn't. I needed to be strong for my Mother and family. This was not a position that I wanted to be in.

I often looked for an escape and refuge from this pain, and I eventually found myself in the arms of a man. I was praying someone would wake me up from this unbearable dream. No one knew what I was going through. I was 27 years old, single, and had given my young adult years to the church.

Friends I previously associated with, didn't understand the change. As a result, we often found ourselves on two different sides of the spectrum. This left me feeling rejected, even more lonely, and confused. I wanted a shoulder to cry on and had none.

Over time, I found a way to run from it all. I ran from my belief systems. I ran from the person everyone thought I was. I became more and more withdrawn. My views started to change. I kept dwelling on why I couldn't just be normal. All my life I wanted to be different and stand out, but not anymore. Not now, and not ever again.

What was worse is that when I ran across people I'd known before, they noticed the sparkle in my eye was gone. Many referenced it, but they had no clue of the pain that was breaking my heart. Often, I found myself trying to explain, but I was often left empty without words.

I was going through an identity crisis. I was caught between wanting to come across as having it all together and letting it all hang out. After serving in the ministry since I was 21, all I wanted to do was simply go somewhere, let my hair down, lick my wounds, and cry.

There are many in the Body of Christ who experience this crisis. They pretend to be strong having it all together when in reality, they are on the verge of a break down. They look to the church for help, only to be disappointed when they find that a temporary service cannot stop the pain.

Others hide behind the mask of who they used to be and resent who they have become. Many are mourning the loss of yesterday without realizing the old man has died, and they are hidden in Christ (Colossians 3:3) with new hope and glory.

IDENTITY

Everywhere my daughter and I go, people call her my "Mini me." Whenever she meets someone from my childhood or we travel to new places, they constantly emphasize how much she looks like me. This isn't because we wear the same clothes or like the same music, it is because she has my DNA.

Hidden in this genetic code are my tendencies, my smile, my exuberance, my feistiness, and everything else that comes with being me. Her dad and I often go back and forth on where she gets her sense of humor or her intelligence. We both know the buck stops with one of us two.

When she was younger I would plant a little seed. I would say, "Where do you come from anyway?" She would look so puzzled. I would say you are supposed to say, "Heaven and God." As she became older the joke was on me.

We would be having a conversation where her growth, beauty, and intelligence would shine through and I would be so taken off guard by some of the things she would say. To quickly deflect, I would ask, "Where do you come from anyway?"

The older she became, she started catching on! She would respond, "You, My Dad, and God!" Ha! My daughter knew her identity. She didn't need anyone to tell her where she came from or who she was connected to. She proudly declared it each and every time.

Although she hadn't grown up with her dad's family, every time she visited them, she was surrounded by familiar character traits, and she proudly smiled. When she came back home, she had a new walk, and a little more confidence. She also started exhibiting a lot more of her Father's tendencies.

This is how the Body of Christ should be. The world should see us and say, "Oh my, you look just like your Father." They should see His characteristics, conversation, and qualities automatically showing up in who we are. The more time we spend with Him, the more apparent it should be.

Identity is important. It lets the world know exactly who you are. It locates where you are, where you are from, and where you belong. In the United States, every citizen is granted certain inalienable rights. These rights are automatically inferred and granted as a benefit. The governments who enforce these rights equitably, do so for the well-being of their citizens.

To access full rights, each citizen must have authorized identification (ID). Police officers called to protect or social welfare programs who distribute resources, demand citizens show their identification. So it is in the Kingdom of God.

Your heavenly identification is hidden in Christ Jesus. Imagine if the only way you could get anything in the Kingdom of God is if you showed your ID card. What if every time you came to God in prayer, He stopped you while you were talking and said, "Wait. Before you ask for one more thing, I need to see your identification."

What if in order to access the word of God when you opened the bible, your identification card was available to be scanned immediately? Where would that leave the church? Guess what? That is exactly how God's kingdom has been established.

JOHN 10:9-11 KJV

9 I am the door: by me if any man enter in, he shall be saved, and shall go in and out, and find pasture.

10 The thief cometh not, but for to steal, and to kill, and to destroy: I am come that they might have life, and that they might have it more abundantly.

11 I am the good shepherd: the good shepherd giveth his life for the sheep.

JESUS CHRIST IS your identity card. Following his footsteps, manifesting sonship, pleasing the Father, and asking in his name is the key that unlocks every door in the Kingdom. It lets fellow citizens, the kingdom of darkness, angels, powers, principalities, and rulers know exactly who they're dealing with. Guess what? We win every time in Him!

It mandates that kingdom laws be enforced. It dictates the laws and rights that govern your life. Your identity in Christ also goes a step further: Enforcing Christ's identification in you also begins to forever embroider and emboss his image.

IMAGE

"Image is nothing, thirst is everything." As I began to prepare for the next youth conference, this Pepsi theme popped into my mind. Remember this was over 20 years ago when social channels like Facebook, Instagram, and Twitter didn't yet exist.

I knew then that young people's worlds were being painted by what they heard and saw. Others often joked about me being too deep. It was the reason I never listened to certain music or sang certain songs. I realized that family background, friends, surroundings, experience, thoughts, and words create our image.

Everyone is talking about it now: How we see ourselves determines what we believe and what we will do. This is why vision boards and affirmations are valuable tools in realigning our perceptions of who we are, what we have to offer, and what we can do.

In my book Voiceprint, I share my personal success formula: vision + voice = velocity. Many have been slowed down because of the image in their own mind or the image others have created for them. Personally, I went through this myself. I had been rejected so much that I started to change. I started to reject who God had made me.

At one time, I was very vocal. I became silent. I was muzzled. I felt handicapped. I couldn't move. Even when I wanted to say or do something different, I found myself on a broken record of repeat and replay. I started listening to and hearing the voices of others. My own voiceprint had become drowned out.

I knew God had a special call on my life since I was young. There were too many instances where God's hand or favor showed up. There were too many confirmations of who He was calling me to be. However, when those I loved the most weren't accepting who I was or had no confidence in what I said, I started to lose confidence in myself.

We, as Christians, don't often confront rejection from a biblical perspective. We talk about how Christ was rejected, but we gloss over it. We make people believe that in order to operate in the fullness of

God, we have to be accepted and liked by people. This is absolutely not true!

As a matter of fact, this is what God has to say:

LUKE 6:22-26 KJV

22 Blessed are ye, when men shall hate you, and when they shall separate you from their company, and shall reproach you, and cast out your name as evil, for the Son of man's sake.

23 Rejoice ye in that day, and leap for joy: for, behold, your reward is great in heaven: for in the like manner did their fathers unto the prophets.

24 But woe unto you that are rich! for ye have received your consolation.

25 Woe unto you that are full! for ye shall hunger. Woe unto you that laugh now! for ye shall mourn and weep.

26 Woe unto you, when all men shall speak well of you! for so did their fathers to the false prophets.

WE, as believers, need to get back to bible basics. If you're reading this, just look in the mirror and say, "Don't get it twisted!"

Don't get it twisted. We were not made to be loved, liked, or accepted by the world. As a matter of fact, the more we look and sound like the Father, the more the world will hate us. Jesus said Satan wished he could "sift Peter out."

Why? Because Peter started walking like Jesus. He started talking like Jesus. At midnight hour, when he was heard praying, he started to sound like Jesus. He had a different language all together. He used to be just a fisherman, but now he was transformed and changed!

There ought to be a distinct difference between us and the world. I am not talking about that difference that says, "I am holier than thou." I don't mean the difference where we isolate ourselves and act better than those around us. I mean the difference that when we speak the world hears God speak. When we pray, things happen, shift, and change. It is time for the sons of God to arise!

Jesus was a disrupter. He was breaking up the old order and bringing a new one. He was declaring, "The Kingdom is at Hand" everywhere he went. They were so afraid of Jesus they didn't want him to open his mouth. They were not sure of what he would declare or say.

When Jesus showed up, the atmosphere began to change. Trees that had a fruitless life started drying up. The poor and sick that had been profited off of for generations began to get healed. The temple that had been exchanging all the money started to be destroyed.

Jesus was confident. He was bold. He was walking in the fullness of God's power. He was the Kingdom of God manifesting heaven on earth. He was a bonafide, authenticated true, tested, tried, and triumphant son.

His own couldn't receive from him because of the image they had built of Jesus in their own minds. This was a false image.

MATTHEW 13:54-58 KJV

54 And when he was come into his own country, he taught them in their synagogue, insomuch that they were astonished, and said, Whence hath this man this wisdom, and these mighty works?

55 Is not this the carpenter's son? is not his mother called Mary? and his brethren, James, and Joses, and Simon, and Judas?

56 And his sisters, are they not all with us? Whence then hath this man all these things?

57 And they were offended in him. But Jesus said unto them, A prophet is not without honour, save in his own country, and in his own house.

58 And he did not many mighty works there because of their unbelief.

JESUS OWN KINFOLK couldn't get the deliverance or healing they needed because of how they saw the son of the Living God. Their image was misconstrued. They heard the authority. They heard the wisdom. They saw the mighty acts, but they couldn't shake their own perceptions and imaginations.

2 CORINTHIANS 10:4-5 KJV

4 (For the weapons of our warfare are not carnal, but mighty through God to the pulling down of strong holds;)

5 Casting down imaginations, and every high thing that exalteth itself against the knowledge of God, and bringing into captivity every thought to the obedience of Christ;

IT's time to shake your perceptions of others and your image of who you are. It may be blocking you from seeing the very person or way God wants to bless you. Arise! Get your healing. Get your healing! See Jesus Christ as He was and is. He was crucified unto death, but rose again for you so you too can arise, take by force, take back and dominate. Arise!

Now more than ever, is the time to see yourself created in the image and likeness of God. See yourself as an extension of the Father. See yourself as one of his most valuable, powerful, living creations. You have dominion on the earth!

Everyone is advocating for animals, a plant-based diet, and saving the environment. I am 100% for walking in wisdom and stewardship, but do you know who you are? It is like a parent having a family dog and a baby. You are not going to give those two creations the same place in your life.

If you die tomorrow, the child is going to get the inheritance. If you die, the child is going to get the house. The child carries your name. The child has your features. The child will be the one to oversee all you have and all you are. The child carries on your legacy. So must we as the sons of the true and living God!

INHERITANCE

The reason many have a hard time accepting the position of a son is because they don't realize what's at stake. The earth is hanging in the balance waiting for you. What's the hold up? Haven't you heard about your inheritance package?

I grew up in the church. You will hear me say this over and over again. Not because I feel like someone given an elite privilege. I repeat this because you can be in church, reading your bible, getting on your knees every day, and still miss the simplest things.

God speaks through the heart. The heart has to be open to receive. The heart has to be tender, pliable, and tilled into good ground. So, going to church for years and years does not make anybody an expert. Certain things have to be revealed by God's Spirit.

Your inheritance is one of those things. For years I knew I had a divine calling, but I didn't see how it was attached to my inheritance. My mother told me years ago when I was about 20 years old, she had a vision of me while we were in church.

Praise was going forth. We were singing, dancing, and having a good time. Those who knew me in high school and in church, know dancing and praising are my thing. I would dance all night until the sweat beads came. It was no different when I gave my life fully over to God and went to church.

They would pass the microphone. I would rap by divine inspiration when asked, play the tambourine when God was moving, and dance all over the church whenever I felt led. This time was not any different. The only thing peculiar was the vision she shared.

She said, "God showed her my portion in heaven." She went on to say, "God said it was "Lonna's blessing." To be honest at the time, I didn't understand it all. She mentioned people and what God showed her about my portion in the kingdom.

I was so young then and it was far over my head, but I never forgot. I always believed God even when I didn't see it or understand. In 1999 when I recorded my first indie project, I threw a release party. The theme was "Lonna's Blessing."

It was a huge success. Now, that I am finally surrendering to the will of God, I see it had nothing to do with that night at all. My inheritance is far bigger than that. It is tied to my acceptance of the call and sonship of God on my life. It is literally stored up in heaven.

Our inheritance is waiting to be released. It can only be exposed after we claim our identity, change our image, and confess, "Lord not my will, but thine be done."

Jesus walked the earth for 33 years when his inheritance was finally released. God had been speaking to him since he was a child. At 12, Jesus was in the temple being about his Father's business.

He was baptized by John. The Holy Spirit descended like a dove. God said, "This is my son in whom I am well pleased. Later, he was tempted in the wilderness and He passed the test.

At this point, Jesus knew who he was. He had already been affirmed by the Father. God had already separated him for his purposes. Yet, Jesus still had to be tested, die, and be resurrected to access his heavenly sonship.

When Jesus died to his own will, plan, and purposes God would give him his rightful seat at his right hand. He would then be "Seated in Heavenly places (Ephesians 2:6) far above powers, principalities, rulers of the darkness of this world, and spiritual wickedness in high places" (Ephesians 1:21).

We too have to die to our ideas, thoughts, perceptions, and future plans. For some it is an easy surrender. For others like me, it may be a 20-year process. We can be misled and believe we have fully surrendered when we have not.

- *How do you know?*
- *Are you still holding on to yesterday?*
- *Are you still wondering what was and what could have been?*
- *Do you still hold grudges against those who you were called to serve?*
- *Are you more concerned with how others see you than how God does?*

- *Do you know you are really supposed to be walking in full-time purpose, but have been staying in the comfort zone?*

All these are signs and symptoms of someone still not ready to surrender to claim their sonship. If you haven't claimed your sonship, you can't get access to your inheritance. In order for Jesus to get to this place of surrender, he had to go to the Garden of Gethsemane.

MATTHEW 26:36-45 KJV

36 Then cometh Jesus with them unto a place called Gethsemane, and saith unto the disciples, Sit ye here, while I go and pray yonder.

37 And he took with him Peter and the two sons of Zebedee, and began to be sorrowful and very heavy.

38 Then saith he unto them, My soul is exceeding sorrowful, even unto death: tarry ye here, and watch with me.

39 And he went a little farther, and fell on his face, and prayed, saying, O my Father, if it be possible, let this cup pass from me: nevertheless not as I will, but as thou wilt.

40 And he cometh unto the disciples, and findeth them asleep, and saith unto Peter, What, could ye not watch with me one hour?

41 Watch and pray, that ye enter not into temptation: the spirit indeed is willing, but the flesh is weak.

42 He went away again the second time, and prayed, saying, O my Father, if this cup may not pass away from me, except I drink it, thy will be done.

43 And he came and found them asleep again: for their eyes were heavy.

44 And he left them, and went away again, and prayed the third time, saying the same words.

45 Then cometh he to his disciples, and saith unto them, Sleep on now, and take your rest: behold, the hour is at hand, and the Son of man is betrayed into the hands of sinners.

· · ·

Notice in the text, Jesus goes to the Garden. Man's original sin also took place in the garden. This time, instead of it being the Garden of Eden, it is the Garden of Gethsamane. Jesus takes three of his disciples with him and His purpose is to pray.

Jesus seeks God's face specifically about his will. Mind you he is not in complete and total surrender, as He petitions God all night. He approaches God three separate times. Each time he ends saying, "Not my will, but thy will be done."

I need you to see this. Jesus wrestles with what is about to happen all night long. His closest confidantes fall asleep on their watch. His enemy is coming to take him out. His defenses are down, and his only defense is God.

When he is going through this spiritual warfare and exchange, the text refers to him as the "Son of man" because Jesus has not yet ascended to his rightful position and seat of power on His heavenly throne, although God has already affirmed him. He is still fighting a fleshly battle on the inside with his image and identity.

He knows God has given him all authority in his hands. He knows he is going to have all power seated next to the King of Kings, but nobody else does. A select few get a glimpse into the coming kingdom. They understand his authority.

Demons have been crying out recognizing who He is. Satan has already put a plan in place to stop him from impacting more people and touching more lives. His disciples have already been arguing about who will have a position closest to Him when He comes into His inheritance. In a few hours, people will be mocking Him saying, "The King of the Jews." Yet, Jesus is still wrestling with the fullness of his sonship.

Up until this moment, Jesus has been declaring the works of His father. He has been referring to Himself as the son. He has publicly made this proclamation, but now His public proclamation is going to be tested.

Now, the word He put out about who He is will come under full persecution. Now, His disciples who have always had His back will be scattered, and He will have to face this alone. His death is necessary to access His heavenly inheritance.

After the third prayer, Jesus finally surrenders. He has prayed all night and God has been building up his faith. God has been talking to Him about how powerful His inheritance is. God has been showing Him that his inheritance will help save, free, and deliver other people.

Jesus is no longer the Son of Man, he has now mentally ascended, transcended, and transformed into the Son of God! We must die to ourselves to claim our rightful inheritance. Our inheritance is tied to helping others. It is generally not about us at all. It glorifies God and glorifies His kingdom.

When we access our full inheritance our personal image and reputation has to be crucified. Who we say we are has to be tested. What we say we are has to be tried. We have to fully die to ourselves.

LUKE 9:20-27 KJV

20 He said unto them, But whom say ye that I am? Peter answering said, The Christ of God.

21 And he straitly charged them, and commanded them to tell no man that thing;

22 Saying, The Son of man must suffer many things, and be rejected of the elders and chief priests and scribes, and be slain, and be raised the third day.

23 And he said to them all, If any man will come after me, let him deny himself, and take up his cross daily, and follow me.

24 For whosoever will save his life shall lose it: but whosoever will lose his life for my sake, the same shall save it.

25 For what is a man advantaged, if he gain the whole world, and lose himself, or be cast away?

26 For whosoever shall be ashamed of me and of my words, of him shall the Son of man be ashamed, when he shall come in his own glory, and in his Father's, and of the holy angels.

27 But I tell you of a truth, there be some standing here, which shall not taste of death, till they see the kingdom of God.

. . .

JESUS UNDERSTOOD what was at stake. He recognized that a nation was depending on him. He realized generations had been praying for years for his arrival. He realized that his death and obedience meant the manifestation of a new kingdom order was ready to be enforced.

Jesus understood the principle that most believers fail to embrace:

JOHN 12:24-25 KJV

24 Verily, verily, I say unto you, Except a corn of wheat fall into the ground and die, it abideth alone: but if it die, it bringeth forth much fruit.

25 He that loveth his life shall lose it; and he that hateth his life in this world shall keep it unto life eternal.

- *Who do men say you are?*
- *Do you still care?*
- *Are you still resisting and fighting against the persecution?*
- *Do you care more about your reputation than you do about the will of God?*
- *Do your friends and social status mean more to you than fulfilling God's promises.*
- *Are you more consumed with your own agenda than God's plan to bring someone else out?*
- *Do your family and friends mean more to you than feeding God's sheep?*

IF YOUR ANSWERS to these questions produced anything more than complete submission to the will of God, then there are parts of you that still need to be crucified and yielded to God.

After Jesus endured the cross, was buried, and rose again, he received five things:

1. **A crown**
2. **A robe**

3. **A ring**
4. **A throne**
5. **A full inheritance**

A CROWN

As sons we have been given a crown. This crown has many different aspects to it. The bible details each in full.
Attributes are:

- Royalty
- Life
- Glory
- Righteousness
- Gold
- Favor
- Holiness
- Anointing Oil
- Flourishing
- Riches
- Incorruptibility

We have a crown. The crown is liable to show up at any time in any form. Wear your crown! When you have time, I encourage you to spend some time in God's word meditating on what it means to carry your crown.

Gold can be weighty and heavy at times. It costs something. It will make you stand out when you want to blend in with a crowd and hide. It can be dark as the night outside, and when you show up wearing your crown, it looks like the rising of the sun. Never forget your crown.

Thomas Whitfield wrote a song called "I shall wear a crown."

THE OLD FOLKS **used to sing it. It goes like this:**

Watch ye, therefore, you know not the day
When the Lord shall call your soul away
If you labor, strivin' for the right,
You shall wear a robe and crown.
Watch ye, therefore, you know not the day
When the Lord shall call your soul away
If you labor, strivin' for the right,
You shall wear a robe and crown.

TOO MANY ARE WALKING around with their head bowed down. They haven't accepted the calling and responsibility that comes with Sonship. Make a decision to access your full inheritance today. God's promises are waiting on you. You are to wear your crown at all times. The world needs to know exactly whose you are and who you are!

A ROBE

As Jesus was being prepared for his journey on the cross, he was given a crown of thorns and a purple robe. Throughout the bible, we see instances of sons being mantled with distinguishable traits and garments to represent the King and his Kingdom.

Aaron, the priest, and his sons were given a robe. Jonathon stripped himself of his own Father's robe and gave it to David. David cut off the skirt of King Saul's robe and spared his life. Joseph had been given a garment of many colors, which also represents a Father's robe or mantle.

THE ROBE REPRESENTS:

- *Authority*
- *Government*
- *An extension of the kingdom*

- *Glory*
- *Righteousness*
- *Judgment*
- *Holiness*
- *Praise*
- *Salvation*
- *Christ*

Put on your robe. A Lot of us have been out here with our you know what hanging out. I can say that because I have done this many times. It's because we've been uncovered. Every day we get up, we have to put Christ on.

When the world sees us, they should see God. As the world sees God, their image of who we are begins to change and so do we. We no longer see ourselves as weak, timid, fearful beings bowing to the whims of another's agenda.

We rise up in strength knowing we have Heaven's full arsenal and kingdom backing us up! We no longer shrink back from who we are, but we fully own up to it. Although Jesus was on his way to the cross, he was clothed in a purple robe.

PURPLE REPRESENTS:

- *Authority*
- *Wealth*
- *Divinity*
- *Majesty*
- *Royalty*
- *Creativity*

ANYONE WHO STUDIES Japanese culture or believes in "Feng Shui" knows that purple represents love. In America, we associate love with the color red for passion. The Japanese design their space and life to correlate with certain colors. They recommend the color purple for the bedroom. Purple also represents the highest form of intimacy one can have with God.

Intimacy with God produces sonship or sons. Sons come forth being birthed out of intimate times in the presence of the Father. You can't manifest God's identity, image, or inheritance on earth as it is in heaven if you haven't spent intimate times in solitude and isolation with him.

These times of intimacy are the only times we should be uncovered and naked. It is the only real place sons have to show their wounds and scars. It is the only true sacred space where sons can let down their hair or let down their guard. It is in this place sons are made and given the strength to arise.

Put on your robe. Never leave home without it. Don't let the world catch you uncovered and naked. They want nothing more than to mock the Father, talk about their experience, have a good time and laugh. Let God cover you with his majesty, divinity, authority, wisdom, providence, and love. He is waiting on you.

A RING

I am a single mother. I always tell my child the story of what attracted me to her Father. As I shared, I had grown up in the church. I always prided myself on celibacy. Even when I wasn't perfect, I still held this value over the years.

When I met my daughter's Father, he was a preacher's son. He wasn't my type at all. It was after my Mother's brain aneurysm. I was going through a lonely time.

We were in a long-distance relationship. He lived far away and was really kind. Since I didn't have cable, he would record sermons for me and mail them. We would talk about the bible. I could laugh with him and be myself. I didn't have to put on airs.

At church, I felt like no one really knew me. Everyone had this perception of me that I was so strong. Yes, I was strong, but it wasn't because I wanted to be. I always had a very bubbly personality. I loved to laugh and let down my hair. I've always hated having to pretend to be something I am really not.

People have always made assumptions. I am highly extroverted, but also highly introverted at times. When people would really get to know me and hear the stories of what I'd been through, they would say things like, "You look so unscathed."

With my daughter's father, I didn't have to pretend. He was as raw, uncut, and real as they came. He was a church musician, so he had seen it all too. We dated for months before he came to visit.

I have fond memories of the few days we spent together. When I went to drop him off at the train station, we pulled up. As he went to get out the car, he asked, "Can I have a kiss?" I responded so quickly and defensively, "I don't kiss just anybody and I don't see a ring on my finger."

I dodged a bullet. I was so proud of myself. His quick thinking completely caught me off guard. He took the ring off his finger, put it on my hand, and said, "Now, there's your ring. Now what?" I was completely in shock and without words.

Looking back, I always laugh. That ring was so special to me. I went and had it resized to fit my hand. I wore it until the day we went our separate ways. You see in my mind, the ring had significant meaning.

I had always said that if my husband ever proposed to me, it wouldn't matter if the ring came from a cracker jack box, I would gladly accept because any man that had the boldness to get through all my resistance and humble himself on one knee, was the man for me. To this day it has never happened and with the sonship call on my life, I am not sure it ever will. We'll see.

That ring meant everything to me. Every time I looked at it, I was reminded of him. It always was a symbol of our commitment even with the miles apart. When his family saw me wearing it, they recognized who it came from. It was one of his most valuable possessions, he had entrusted me with and given to me.

In our culture, a ring represents the united of two souls. It represents a covenant and a promise. In the bible, when a king gave his decree, it was sealed using a signet from his ring. In the book of Genesis, when Pharaoh gave Joseph authority, he sealed the deal by handing him his signet ring.

A RING REPRESENTS:

- Access to the Father
- Approval and affirmation
- Authority
- Divine connection
- Divine decree
- Oneness
- Rank
- Royalty
- Valuable treasure
- Weight and glory

IN MARRIAGE, a ring is the final exchange before sealing the deal. When Jesus went to the cross, died and rose again, he sealed the deal for all humanity. Now, we have access to our heavenly inheritance. We've been given the keys to unlock the kingdom.

A THRONE

When Jesus was resurrected, he rose to take his rightful seat of authority at the right hand of God. First born children are historically known to be their Father's right hand. Benjamin, Israel's youngest literally meant "Son of my right hand." Sonship is a matter of positioning.

Scripture tells us where this right hand of authority is located. It resides in heavenly places.

EPHESIANS 1:19-23 KJV

19 And what is the exceeding greatness of his power to us-ward who believe, according to the working of his mighty power,

20 Which he wrought in Christ, when he raised him from the dead, and set him at his own right hand in the heavenly places,

21 Far above all principality, and power, and might, and dominion, and every name that is named, not only in this world, but also in that which is to come:

22 And hath put all things under his feet, and gave him to be the head over all things to the church,

23 Which is his body, the fulness of him that filleth all in all.

THRONES REPRESENT DOMINION. They are a seat of authority God allows a ruler to rule from. Every king since the beginning of time is responsible for a certain domain. This domain is governed by laws, principles, and has domiciles within.

The king or ruler reigning on a throne, governs and is responsible for the commonwealth of its people. The king or ruler also has royal subjects who submit to his or her command. Jesus obeyed God until death.

His submission pleased the Father. As a result, he gave him a name above every other name that is named. In conjunction with your heavenly father, Jesus Christ rules on the throne over all. Jesus in his lovingkindness, didn't just come to take possession of the throne for His Father. He came to take back possession for all mankind.

ROMANS 8:14-17 KJV

14 For as many as are led by the Spirit of God, they are the sons of God.

15 For ye have not received the spirit of bondage again to fear; but ye have received the Spirit of adoption, whereby we cry, Abba, Father.

16 The Spirit itself beareth witness with our spirit, that we are the children of God:

17 And if children, then heirs; heirs of God, and joint-heirs with Christ; if so be that we suffer with him, that we may be also glorified together.

ONCE WE ACCEPT our position as sons, we become joint-heirs of God (Romans 8:17). We have access to His Spirit, promises, redemption, and our full inheritance. We can reign from a position of authority, dominion, power, wisdom, and rank over all things.

When Jesus came to the earth, the children of Israel were not in a position to recognize his sonship. Ever since Israel had become a nation, all they had known was a leader or a king. Jesus came demonstrating and speaking of a higher kingdom.

Many are so used to needing something else to govern, lead, or rule their lives. This is why we, as believers, often miss the revelation of sonship. When you submit yourself fully as God's son, God has the first and final say. What He says goes. What He says do, you do. Even at times, when this comes with persecution, suffering, and pain.

When you reign from a God appointed throne, you don't have time to complain. You aren't somewhere at home licking your wounds. You are humbled, positioned for the Father to speak, have access to your life, and give his command at any time. After you have been fully clothed in Christ and seated on your Father's throne, it's time to receive, walk in, and access your inheritance.

A FULL INHERITANCE PACKAGE

I must admit. Up until recently, I didn't really understand the value of having an inheritance. I grew up in a single parent household. My father traveled the world preaching and teaching. My Mother raised us with God's help and alone.

I will say my Father did do his best to prepare us for his departure. He planned over 20 years in advance. I appreciate the steps he took to make sure we didn't carry the weight and burden of his funeral. More than anything, he wanted his children to have access to whatever he had accumulated.

In 2017, when we buried him, it didn't seem like he had done that much. However, as I meditated on the care and precision that went into the planning, my perspective has evolved. I listen to Dr. Bill Winston and have streamed his service for years. I also attended several of his business and leadership conferences.

I would often hear him talking about getting your inheritance package. At first, it sounded like something over my head. Inheritance package? Really? Where? I wanted to know so I could cash in. I thought it may be pie in the sky, but after all I had been through I was willing to believe.

Anyone that knows Dr. Winston knows everything he does is biblically based. From my experience, if it's not in the book, he doesn't say it. I kept listening and pondering this inheritance package building my faith.

Then, one day, listening to one of his ministers, Dr. Tiffany K. Jordan, she gave the scripture. I was in total shock and surprise. After everything the Lord had revealed to me, how could I have just skipped past this verse!

REVELATION 5:12-13 KJV

12 Saying with a loud voice, Worthy is the Lamb that was slain to receive power, and riches, and wisdom, and strength, and honour, and glory, and blessing.

13 And every creature which is in heaven, and on the earth, and under the earth, and such as are in the sea, and all that are in them, heard I saying, Blessing, and honour, and glory, and power, be unto him that sitteth upon the throne, and unto the Lamb for ever and ever.

Now, you might be like me. You might be hesitant to take full possession. It is only according to your faith that you can receive. Not only that, you also have to be a son first before you can even attain this level of faith.

I can assure you, although hard to believe, God's promises are "Yes and amen" (2 Corinthians 1:20). God says in His word, "line upon line and precept upon precept" (Isaiah 28:10, 13). He also leaves a pattern and says, "Out of the mouth of two or three witnesses let everything be confirmed" (Deuteronomy 19:15, Matthew 18:16, 2 Corinthians 13:1, 1 Timothy 5:19, Hebrews 10:28).

John confirms our inheritance when writing the book of Revelation. Paul has already clearly outlined and detailed our inheritance and estate rights in Ephesians 1.

EPHESIANS 1:10-14 KJV

10 That in the dispensation of the fulness of times he might gather together in one all things in Christ, both which are in heaven, and which are on earth; even in him:

11 In whom also we have obtained an inheritance, being predestined according to the purpose of him who worketh all things after the counsel of his own will:

12 That we should be to the praise of his glory, who first trusted in Christ.

13 In whom ye also trusted, after that ye heard the word of truth, the gospel of your salvation: in whom also after that ye believed, ye were sealed with that holy Spirit of promise,

14 Which is the earnest of our inheritance until the redemption of the purchased possession, unto the praise of his glory.

As JOINT HEIRS and Sons of God, we have an inheritance package. It's up to us to claim it—it has everything we need to be victorious in this life and beyond. Our heavenly Father has given us His kingdom and the world for our possession. It's time to arise and take our portion.

The only way to fully get what belongs to us is to die to the past and ourselves. We can no longer afford to wrestle with God. He is looking for His investment. He is seeking joint heirs to help establish and reign on His throne.

We must make a decision to find our identity in Him alone. We must behold His face, allowing Him to transform us into His image and likeness. Once we do, we will be equipped to bring His message of forgiveness, love, triumph, deliverance, healing, and blessing to a dying world.

We are not waiting on God. God is waiting on us. The time to manifest is NOW! "Now are we the Sons of God" (1 John 3:2). There are many dimensions and characteristics of the Father. This is why it takes a walk of consistency and faith to get to know Him. We, as Sons, can only manifest what we know. What is revealed, we are to manifest "NOW!"

BORN TO REIGN

⚜

As we dominate the earth as Sons, our confidence must arise. We must walk with a boldness and assurance knowing we have been affirmed. In this life, our faith will be tried. This trying of faith is to perfect our patience and the Father's perfect work in us.

Our heavenly Father automatically sets us up for success. When we accept Jesus Christ as our Lord and Savior, our genetic code demands we rule and win. We cannot fail.

Through the baptism and filling of His Holy Spirit we grow to know the Father more and more every day. Sometimes this journey takes us on the path of the unknown. This uncertainty tests us. It presents circumstances, obstacles, and setbacks to make one waiver and doubt.

What an authentic Son of God must know, is that the fight is fixed. He or she must keep their eyes on the promise. We cannot allow ourselves to get distracted or deterred by what we see around us. We are born to win!

When I first found out I was pregnant with my daughter, so many thoughts went through my head. I wanted to be the best mother and give her the world. My own Mother had given us girls so much. She literally trained us how to be God fearing, virtuous women.

When we grew older, she opened a store in the mall called, "Women of Virtues." She wanted to show women all the things they could do, accomplish, and be through the word of God. My Mother was my rock and best friend. When she had her brain aneurysm and stroke, I didn't leave the hospital for the first three weeks, while her life lay hanging in the balance.

She was intubated in intensive care and induced into a coma to keep the aneurysm from hemorrhaging. I remember watching the breathing machines, at times wanting to get in the bed to lay beside her. I wanted her to hear my heart beat and feel my love.

After five long months and tear drenched fasting and prayers, my Mother came home. The entire experience from her being admitted to her discharge and beyond, was a true humbling and testing of my family's faith.

Within three years of my Mother's accident, my child's Father and I learned the news. I was having my first child. This in itself was a miracle since I had always prayed I wouldn't have children. I didn't want to bring a child into this dark, cold world.

I had a very close friend named Clara Grayson who would always tell me, "I was going to have a child and that would change." Well, after getting older and pouring my life into my church with seemingly very little to show for it, it did. So, when I found out I was having a little girl, my life changed.

I remember thinking about my Mother. She couldn't counsel us anymore. She couldn't pray for us like she used to, or be there when things were out of sorts. I started thinking about how to make sure my daughter had everything she needed, even if something happened and I wasn't here.

I created a list of everything I wanted for her and wanted her to know. I also wrote a list of all my hopes and dreams for her. I wanted her to know my heart regardless of the future. I wanted to ensure she was set up for success and equipped for whatever lay ahead.

This is the Father's heart for us. When we are truly born into the kingdom, He knows there will be rocky roads ahead, and He has equipped us with everything we need to become just like Him. We have been encoded with His life, power, wisdom, spirit and more. All He wants us to do is trust and believe in Him.

Although we are Sons of God, he still knows our frailties. He understands our weaknesses. His strength comes to make us strong. We don't have to hide from God. Ever! The Father knows right where we are at all times. The GPS of His Spirit can locate us in a moment's time.

PSALMS 139:7-18 KJV

7 Whither shall I go from thy spirit? or whither shall I flee from thy presence?

8 If I ascend up into heaven, thou art there: if I make my bed in hell, behold, thou art there.

9 If I take the wings of the morning, and dwell in the uttermost parts of the sea;

10 Even there shall thy hand lead me, and thy right hand shall hold me.

11 If I say, Surely the darkness shall cover me; even the night shall be light about me.

12 Yea, the darkness hideth not from thee; but the night shineth as the day: the darkness and the light are both alike to thee.

13 For thou hast possessed my reins: thou hast covered me in my mother's womb.

14 I will praise thee; for I am fearfully and wonderfully made: marvellous are thy works; and that my soul knoweth right well.

15 My substance was not hid from thee, when I was made in secret, and curiously wrought in the lowest parts of the earth.

16 Thine eyes did see my substance, yet being unperfect; and in thy book all my members were written, which in continuance were fashioned, when as yet there was none of them.

17 How precious also are thy thoughts unto me, O God! how great is the sum of them!

18 If I should count them, they are more in number than the sand: when I awake, I am still with thee.

. . .

IT AMAZES me when people hide from God. How can you hide from He that was, is, and is to come? How can you hide from the Creator and Possessor of heaven and earth? How can you possibly hide from Him that formed you and fashioned you in your Mother's womb?

Newsflash, you can't!

So, when you are going through the fire, that is the time to rejoice and be glad knowing He is right in it with you. No matter the sin and hell you've been through, God was there the entire time. I remember when God gave me this revelation in my own life.

I literally felt like I was going through hell. Some would say it was because of bad choices. Honestly, I don't know. I honestly think there were times when the enemy just literally wanted to annihilate my faith, but it didn't work!

The DNA of God kept bringing me back to life every time. I remember when He started showing and talking to me about the power of the cross and what Jesus did. He literally went to hell for three days. He hung out. He was surrounded by death, filth, and stinch.

He was hanging out in prison with them and was STILL PREACHING!

He didn't stop preaching while he was in hell!

As a matter of fact, HE PREACHED LOUDER!

He knew his hour had come. He knew the closer the three-day expiration period came, he was about to have all dominion in heaven and earth in his hands.

He was going to be with the Father. Right in hell, Jesus was a preaching machine. He was born to reign! If that doesn't make you smile, what will? You have been given a promise of peace and a chosen outcome that says, "You win!" The fight is fixed!

So, the question is this. What are we as Sons supposed to do in the meantime? What do we do in the time in between being born into the Kingdom and our death, burial, and resurrection? "We Walk it out!"

Do you know that secular song? The chorus just says, "Walk it out!" That's it. You have to just keep walking, living, moving, breathing, and hoping by faith. God is and is not looking for perfection at the same time.

I am working on a new book titled, "Flawless." You see in this world that's what perfection means. Hollywood and the media makes us believe that in order to get the shares, likes, and followers, we have to be flawless. It makes us embrace the false, temporary, and that which deceives.

God is not looking for that kind of perfection. The kind He is looking for is maturity.

LUKE 6:40 KJV

40 The disciple is not above his master: but every one that is perfect shall be as his master.

IN THIS PASSAGE, when Jesus is talking about being "perfect," he is talking about becoming mature in God. So many are in one of three stages in their personal walk with God:

1. **They have been raised in the church.** Church is all they have known. They speak churchese (the jargon church people use when speaking with one another), but are oblivious to what's happening in the world. These, and I can speak from experience, are those who are "So heavenly minded they are no earthly good."
2. **There are also those who are born into the Kingdom without knowing anything about God at all.** They have a passion, hunger, and thirst to know more, but may have a "Zeal without knowledge (Romans 10:2)." These may get turned off by churchese. They just want God in His simplest form.
3. **Then there are those that may be mature, understanding**

the deep things of God. Either they've been called to leadership, or are somewhere just holding on to someone else's deliverance not comfortable with status quo. They also may not currently see a place for them in the physical church structure that currently exists.

4. **Then there are leaders who bear the responsibility and weight of carrying others** who may not be equipped with the knowledge and skill to duplicate themselves.

5. **There are also those with nontraditional gifts** who because the church has not focused on these gifts, may not have any leadership roles at all.

REGARDLESS, of where you fall in the spectrum, when you're born into the Kingdom of God, you are given dietary restrictions. Either you are on milk or meat. If you are on milk, you are supposed to nurse from the Spirit of God and those who have the ability to cultivate and nurture the gift inside. If you are transitioning from milk to meat. It is time for you to get weaned and come, "Off the bottle."

Yes. There may be a period of adjustment. Now, your digestive system has to really kick in. What used to be easy to swallow and went down very smoothly is now going to take some chewing on. It's going to take thinking about it, meditating on it, and breaking it down.

It is imperative that this process takes place in order for the Sons of God to take their rightful place. Sons have been born to reign. However, the Father knows that Sons are ready to take possession of the Kingdom and their throne when they are able to "Eat at the King's table."

This requires a level of maturity. You no longer have to be coddled and pacified. At this stage, you understand God is no longer "Winking at your mess." You grow from needing to be carried to carrying others. You go from murmuring and complaining to "Glorying in your suffering."

This is a tall order, but it is mandatory for every son. You can't be a Son of God whining and complaining about every little thing that comes to shake you. God owns the cattle on a thousand hills (Psalm 50:10), and He is not worried about one thing. As a Son, you shouldn't be either.

God isn't swayed with how things look. He's not even swayed with how you feel. As the King, His decree stands and remains. He wants to know, "Did you hear what I said?" "Son, did you hear what I said?"

We as the people of God need to grow up. I've heard sermon after sermon preached. Very seldom do I ever hear Sons being admonished for the "Little foxes that spoil the vine" (Song of Solomon 2:15). Here are some questions I often quietly think but now would like to openly pose to you:

- *How can you be a Son still putting your mouth on other people?*
- *How can you be a Son turning your nose up at others and the poor?*
- *How can you be a Son talking about how someone is dressed and what they have on?*
- *How can you be a Son gossiping, backbiting, and also offended about the smallest little things?*
- *How can you be a Son competing for position, status, fortune, and fame?*
- *How can you be a Son always needing someone to recognize who you are and needing someone to always stroke your ego?*
- *How can you be a Son using your gifts to curse others instead of to bless?*
- *How can you be a Son?*

You can't be a Son without God's leading, instruction, love, affirmation, and grace. It takes a level of dying to yourself and maturity. I see people lifting up leaders and celebrating their church family, but then shunning and being ashamed of their own families. How can you be a Son when you haven't even followed the mandate found in Isaiah 58? "Will ye call this a fast unto the Lord?" God honors family and works through families.

I CORINTHIANS 13:10-13

10 But when that which is perfect is come, then that which is in part shall be done away.

11 When I was a child, I spake as a child, I understood as a child, I thought as a child: but when I became a man, I put away childish things.

12 For now we see through a glass, darkly; but then face to face: now I know in part; but then shall I know even as also I am known.

13 And now abideth faith, hope, charity, these three; but the greatest of these is charity.

IT IS time to put away childish things (1 Corinthians 13:11). Rise up! You were born to reign. You are destined to be a Son of God. It's time to manifest! The earth is waiting on you.

SHOW UP! SHOW OUT! IT'S YOUR TIME! YOU WERE BORN TO REIGN!

TRANSFORM TO TRANSCEND

*Y*ou are chosen for such a time as this, and it is time for you to take your rightful place. You must take possession of your rightful throne. Someone somewhere is waiting on you. "I am" must become your possession confession!

"You have not, because you ask not" (James 4:3). What are you believing God for? What is your confession of faith? In order to walk in the Sonship dimension, you have to fully ask and possess God's inheritance for you. You can only do so by identifying yourself and declaring, "I am."

Let's start this section off with a few "Possession Confessions:"

- *I am what I am by the grace of God.*
- *I am that I am.*
- *I am called. I am chosen.*
- *I am born to reign.*
- *I am created in the image of the Almighty God.*
- *I am a Son of God.*
- *I am that light that was sent into the world.*
- *I am the bread of life.*

- *I am the living water. If any many drink of me, he will never thirst again.*
- *I am the sent one.*
- *I am the resurrection, and I am life.*
- *I am salt.*
- *I am truth.*
- *I am fearfully and wonderfully made.*
- *I am the true vine and the branches.*
- *I am the door.*
- *I am the good shepherd.*
- *I am bought with a price.*

YOU SEE in order to claim and possess your inheritance as a joint heir, you have to walk and talk like Jesus does. You have to look like him, sound like him, and be like him. You must be "Transformed by the renewing of your mind" (Romans 12:2). "Old things are passed away and behold all things become new" (2 Corinthians 5:17).

So many see Jesus, but don't see themselves in Him. So many preach Jesus as a risen savior. They see a resurrected King, but don't see that same power living on the inside. Jesus came declaring who He was and what He was about.

Some saw Jesus proclaiming "I am," as arrogance or even blasphemy. Jesus' bold statements or what I call, possession confessions, are exactly the reason why the Pharisees and Sadducees wanted to kill him.

Jesus knew that when he spoke, he wasn't simply speaking or conversing with "flesh and blood." He was imitating the likeness of His Father when he created man in the garden. He was speaking, creating, and saying, "Let this be," and it was.

ROMANS 10:8-10 KJV

8 But what saith it? The word is nigh thee, even in thy mouth, and in thy heart: that is, the word of faith, which we preach;

9 That if thou shalt confess with thy mouth the Lord Jesus, and shalt believe in thine heart that God hath raised him from the dead, thou shalt be saved.

10 For with the heart man believeth unto righteousness; and with the mouth confession is made unto salvation.

WHAT IF JESUS would have shrunk back or backed down? What if he would have taken the low road or played small? We wouldn't be repeating and declaring his words thousands of years later. He left a pattern for us to follow to transcend all time, confines, and constraints.

This pattern was repeated in Moses' era and Jesus followed suit. It started with two words, "I am." A believer cannot proclaim they are anything unless they clearly see it first. Once he or she gets a clear picture or image in their mind, they can begin to affect change in themselves and those around them.

I remember in June 2018, I was on a journey to fulfill God's purposes in my life. Suddenly, I found myself in a situation that came out of nowhere. It totally caught me off guard. I was totally broken and devastated. I was weeping, sobbing, and crying out before the Lord.

As I was praying, God quickened my spirit. He said, "That's not how I see you at all." He started flashing scenes of my life before my eyes. Then, He said, "I see you as triumphant." In a moment's time, my thoughts shifted. My perspectives changed. I began to write as I heard Him speak. Here's what I was given:

"I SEE HIM IN ME"

Thank you Lord,
For causing me to see
Every day I wake up and get up,
I am you in the earth.

I am your overcoming power.

I am your resurrecting power.

I am triumph.

I am your work of beauty.

I am someone to be marveled.

I am you God, and you are me.

I overcome.

*I am you Lord seated in Heavenly Places in Christ Jesus "FAR
   ABOVE"*

All:

Principalities
Powers
Dominions
Kingdoms
Thrones,
The rulers of the darkness of this world,
Spiritual wickedness in high places
Kings
Governments,
*And... ALL DOMINIONS... in this life and that which is to
   come.*

I am triumph.

I am triumphant over and over again.

The angels marvel at the work of the Living God in me.

I am beauty. I am beautiful and I see God's handiwork and beauty in me.

I marvel at the beauty of the "Living God"...HIS handiwork, HIS triumphant power, HIS resurrecting power, HIS life, HIS voice, HIS truth, HIS honor, HIS strength, HIS wonder, HIS mercy, HIS grace, HIS glory, and HIS love in me.

I marvel at the tenacity of the "Living God" and HIS overcoming power in me.

God has given me the "Keys of Life" in my hands.

I have them. I possess them at all times, to unlock myself and to unlock others.

To cause the dead to hear.

To cause the blind to see.

To cause the dead to quicken back to life.

To resurrect God's dry bones.

I live. I move. I have my being in Him, and He lives in me.

To do according to HIS great will, HIS pleasure, HIS power, The riches of HIS grace and mercy. I live. I move. I have

*my being in Him at the seat of the right Hand of the
Father. I cannot and will not ever be moved from my
rightful seat of authority in Christ Jesus the Hope of "ALL"
glory... the Resurrected one.*

The Son of the "Living God."

I am a SON!

The earth is groaning and waiting for my full manifestation.

*I am becoming more and more like Him every day and I am
    see HIM
in me, on me, through me, for me, with me and by me every
    step of the way...*

*Every minute
Every second
Every breath...
He is with me, in me, on me, through me, for me, by me and I
    see Him.*

I speak Him. I hear Him. I think Him. I live Him.

YOU SEE MOST of the time it is not what we are going through, but
how we see it. There is always a dimension of God's glory He's
attempting to reveal in us. Everything we go through or grow through
should always point back to Him.

God has always given me a revelation of Sonship and resurrection.
Many times I would just feel such obscurity or hopelessness, but then
I would see Jesus. I'd see Him getting up with all power in his hands.
I'd see Him sitting at the right hand of God.

I'd see Jesus raising Lazarus from the grave. I'd see Him making the sick whole again. I'd see Him multiplying and feeding 5,000. I had personal encounters with the Son. I found my own identity in His.

In my own life, God always reveals Himself as the "King of Kings," and "Lord of Lords." He's always shown me "His triumph." His ability to persevere time and time again. Think back on your life.

- *What has God said to you?*
- *What has He revealed about who you are?*

THROUGHOUT LIFE, I've suffered and endured a lot of persecution. Most times, it's been with the purest intentions on my end. There were also times of crushing, pressing, and correction. God has always been with me every step of the way. He's faithfully led, guided, and taught me through it all.

I'll never forget a powerful church leadership meeting almost 20 years ago. We were in corporate prayer and I saw a vision from God. It happened in an instant. Then, I heard His voice say: "Transform to Transcend."

He literally illuminated my mind. I could clearly see how to ascend to a "Heavenly seat in Christ Jesus." I saw how anyone who transformed into the "Image of Jesus" could transcend any earthly power or place trying to hold them bound. I saw the ability to defy spiritual gravity.

I shared this publicly with the Pastor and entire leadership team. At the time, I was the youngest person in the room. Even as a child and throughout my youth, God always spoke and showed me hidden things. This particular instance was over 20 years ago.

After being fought and resisted many times, I became withdrawn. Speaking out came with so much persecution and pain. What I was saying was not traditional. Yet, I always knew it was 100% God. I was years ahead of my time. There was really no space for a voice like mine.

Concepts shared and revelations given would be viewed as being rebellious, fighting against the head, or sometimes not following leadership. God's Word, Spirit, and Power is not bound to physical space or location. His body is one. When the mouth speaks, everything else listens. Most times, when a word comes from the mouth, it should have already traveled from the brain through the nervous system and meditated upon before it's released.

The truth is when God sends a word or revelation, it is to move His people from one place to another. It is to shift the mindset and thinking. If you're reading this book, God is shifting your mindset. He's shifting the way you view people, places, and things. He's rearranging your thought processes. He's making a new bottle and pouring in new wine.

As this shifting occurs, you must be ready to embrace your "I am." Embracing it, will help you transform to transcend. Transforming into the image and likeness of God is the only way you can ascend. Like Christ, when you ascend you will have dominion over principalities, powers, rulers of darkness, and spiritual wickedness in high places. They will no longer be able to resist you or God's plan.

EPHESIANS 1:18-23 KJV

18 The eyes of your understanding being enlightened; that ye may know what is the hope of his calling, and what the riches of the glory of his inheritance in the saints,

19 And what is the exceeding greatness of his power to us-ward who believe, according to the working of his mighty power,

20 Which he wrought in Christ, when he raised him from the dead, and set him at his own right hand in the heavenly places,

21 Far above all principality, and power, and might, and dominion, and every name that is named, not only in this world, but also in that which is to come:

22 And hath put all things under his feet, and gave him to be the head over all things to the church,

23 Which is his body, the fulness of him that filleth all in all.

. . .

CHANGE HOW YOU SEE YOURSELF. Change how you see yourself in Him. See yourself seated in Him. There were days I had to fight and pray to maintain my seat. Every day, regardless of what was happening in my life, I made a decision that I wasn't coming down off my seat.

I think many times as believers, we tend to abdicate our seat. We change it like we change clothes. This is not what God intended at all. To be seated speaks of remaining, sitting, and taking rest. We must rest in our seat of authority because we are the Sons of God and sonship is not temporary.

We help the Father enforce and oversee His creation. We rule with Him in righteousness. He's faithful and His rule remains forever settled! We can't go on our own strength.

Let's stop hiding behind the four walls of our local church. Let's stop sitting and listening to Sunday sermon after sermon without any real change. We must transform to transcend. The time is now.

IT'S TIME TO MANIFEST

*S*ons of God are rising up across the earth. They are already positioned to take dominion. Romans 8:19 says, the "For the earnest expectation of the creature waiteth for the manifestation of the sons of God." In other words, the whole earth is groaning waiting for the manifestation of the Sons of God." To **manifest** is when something becomes: Clear or obvious to the eye or mind.

Many Sons have been in training. You've waited for outside influences to affirm who you are. You know what you carry. It's time to manifest.

Agree to fully walk in it. No one else can fill your shoes. No one can take your place. You are a piece of God's heart and the apple of His eye.

JOHN 10:28-30 KJV

28 And I give unto them eternal life; and they shall never perish, neither shall any man pluck them out of my hand.

29 My Father, which gave them me, is greater than all; and no man is able to pluck them out of my Father's hand.

30 I and my Father are one.

YOU HAVE A DESTINY TO FULFILL. *You are called and chosen for such a time as this. God has a plan for you.*

JEREMIAH 29:11-14 KJV

11 For I know the thoughts that I think toward you, saith the Lord, thoughts of peace, and not of evil, to give you an expected end.

12 Then shall ye call upon me, and ye shall go and pray unto me, and I will hearken unto you.

13 And ye shall seek me, and find me, when ye shall search for me with all your heart.

14 And I will be found of you, saith the Lord: and I will turn away your captivity, and I will gather you from all the nations, and from all the places whither I have driven you, saith the Lord; and I will bring you again into the place whence I caused you to be carried away captive.

IN MY OWN LIFE, I have failed the Father many times. I have frequently missed the mark. Missing it, took me on an endless path of distractions and destruction that could have been prevented. It took me 20 years to write this book.

The revelations shared, were given to me in prayer. As I prayed for others, God started giving me songs about His kingdom and sonship. I never understood why this revelation came at such a devastating time in my life. The songs helped carry me through really tough times.

When I felt abandoned, lost, or rejected, I would hear God's voice gently singing these songs over me. Even when I didn't feel, look, or act like a son, these songs became my confession of faith.

"Now, are we Sons of God". In this particular song, I heard emphasis on these words:

"It does not yet appear
What we shall be
But we know when He comes
We shall see Him as He is.
We shall be like Him."

THIS SONG IS TAKEN from the scripture found in I John 3:2. As the stanza highlights, it doesn't appear what we shall be. We don't know the fullness of who we are in God until we mature and become everything God has dreamed. We are walking it out becoming the fullness of the Godhead body.

However, we do know that as God reveals Himself to us and through us, we shall be like Him. God wants to use the pages of your book to reveal to the world who He is in you. He wants to turn your story into a best seller and your song into a beautiful love song.

Let Him. Don't be like me. I waited 20 years for someone to validate what the Father was showing me in secret. Whatever He is showing you in secret, He wants to reward you with publicly. Take a step closer toward the Father today.

The hairs on your head are numbered (Matthew 10:30). If you've gone astray, God's been patiently waiting for you. Accept His invitation to come back home. He'll openly welcome you back, even if you're like the Prodigal Son, who took his inheritance prematurely and left.

You still have a reserved spot in the Kingdom with your name on it. Fully come to yourself and recognize who you are. You will always be treated as a Son.

When you show up on the scene, you'll be like Jesus declaring, "The Kingdom of God is at Hand." Jesus always showed up with an announcement. He manifested God's presence and glory each and every time he arrived on the scene. Now, it's your turn.

We must manifest. The world will keep getting darker and darker until we do. We carry and possess a light that pierces the darkness. The darkness does not comprehend it. However, this light causes the earth to respond.

John 1:4-9 KJV

4 In him was life; and the life was the light of men.

5 And the light shineth in darkness; and the darkness comprehended it not.

6 There was a man sent from God, whose name was John.

7 The same came for a witness, to bear witness of the Light, that all men through him might believe.

8 He was not that Light, but was sent to bear witness of that Light.

9 That was the true Light, which lighteth every man that cometh into the world.

YOU ARE that light and life the world needs in this hour. You are the door someone needs to walk through. Jesus is saying, "Won't you join me on the throne?"

There is a divine, predestined inheritance set aside waiting with your name on it. God's best is ready to meet and greet you. Allow the Father to adorn you with His crown, robe, ring, and seal. He is ready to mature you into the fullness of your Glory.

The Father will never let you falter or faint. He will always be there to strengthen you. You have been given divine security detail. He'll make sure you make it to your "Expected end."

PHILLIPIANS 1:6 KJV

6 Being confident of this very thing, that he which hath begun a good work in you will perform it until the day of Jesus Christ.

I AM confident even as I type that God's predestination plan is manifesting right before your eyes. Everything held up is being unlocked.

Everything hidden is being revealed. You are receiving divine wisdom and instruction now for how to move ahead.

Hear the voice of the Father calling you higher. There are higher dimensions of His sonship waiting on you. He is simply waiting for you to make a decision. No more hesitating. It's time to manifest. The world is waiting on you!

Heavenly Father,

I know you have chosen and called me for such a time as this. I boldly declare "I am a son!" Let your kingdom come in my life today. Let your will be eternally done. I rest in your providence, provision, and protection. I rest knowing that your thoughts are only good concerning me. Father, make me a reflection of you in the earth. Transform me into your likeness and image and the image of your dear son. Help me align with your original intent when created man in the garden. I accept your call to sonship. Father, I answer. From today and moving forward, I declare like Jesus, "I am my Father are one." Lord, make us one. Walk with me. Talk with me. Live in me, on me, through me, for me, by me and around me. I proclaim I am bought with a price. I surrender. I am yours.

Forever Your Son,
Amen

AUTHOR'S NOTES

Every year I have the privilege to speak to new audiences around the world to ignite hope and transformation. There is nothing more satisfying than seeing new relationships form, dead dreams come alive, and untapped potential turn to power.

I remember the first time I spoke in front of an audience. I was a 14-year-old Texan with a message for the world. I was born to speak and teach. I love connecting with audiences to share real-world experiences, proven principles, and breakthrough strategies.

I've spent decades inspiring and investing in people. I've challenged the status quo and provoked change with powerful messages that go against conventional wisdom. Whether a Fortune 500 company, educational institution, or nonprofit, my passion is to help others break out-of-the-box to see new possibilities and experience exponential growth.

Thank you for reading this book! When I wrote the book I was in a time of deep reflection. At that time, I realized I was looking in others for what I'd hope to find within. I pray you are inspired to take action and run quickly into the open arms of your Heavenly Father. He's always there to pick us up when we need Him most.

WHO IS LONNA HARDIN

Lonna Hardin is a woman of faith who leads with love, light, and integrity. Through music, the multi-gifted creative educates, speaks, and sings to the souls that are thirsty for God's love and grace, just as she is.

The ambitious single mother from the midwest has experienced many tests and trials, only equipping her to become strengthened in her faith and gracefully transformed into God's image.

Lonna is an authentic Christian leader who honors her Lord and savior and has cultivated many businesses and organizations that embody the visions God has blessed her with to be a blessing to others.

In addition to being an author and inspiration to others, Lonna is a Gospel radio-hit making recording artist who's smooth, sultry voice has been featured on the top 150 U.S. gospel stations around the world. She also received worldwide recognition as #17 on the International Top 30 Artist list.

Now, Lonna sings, writes, and speaks, with audiences around the world. She's also a voice to add light to issues that impact the voiceless and vulnerable.

Lonna is acclaimed author of several books including, 'Voiceprint and the Melody's Song children's book series, as well as a powerful faith-based series. Her books are featured at libraries, bookstores, museums, and and events across the country.

You've seen or heard her inspire on TBN, Black Gospel, Story-telling Companion, and television or radio stations around the world.

Lonna Hardin's high-spirited energy and message of hope is why audiences say they experience the wow factor after hearing Lonna sing or speak at conferences, workshops, seminars, and events. To see Lonna 'Live or book her at your next event, visit lonnahardin.com

Lonna Hardin Enterprises
lonnahardin.com